TOM HANKS BIO
BOOK

The Inside Story Behind the Personal Life,
Movies, Legacy, Net worth, Wives, Why on
Strike and Health Status of the American
Movie Star

VERA J. LESSARD

Copyright Page

Table Of Contents

Introduction

Tom Hanks is a well-known American actor and one of the highest-paid movie stars of all time. His role in Ron Howard's romantic comedy 'Splash' catapulted him to fame. With his roles as Robert Langdon in the films 'The Da Vinci Code' and 'Angels & Demons,' he achieved tremendous commercial success and rose to become one of Hollywood's highest-paid actors. His charm and cheery demeanor gave him immediate recognition, and he was regularly likened to Hollywood icons such as Cary Grant, Henry Fonda, Jimmy Stewart, and Gary Cooper. With films like 'That Thing You Do!' and 'Larry Crowne,' he has established himself not just as an actor, but also as a writer and director. He has produced several films and documentaries, including "From the Earth to the Moon," "Band of Brothers," and "The Pacific." He has received several prizes and distinctions for his outstanding work throughout the years, including seven 'Primetime Emmy prizes,' two 'Academy Awards,' a 'Tony Award,' a 'Legion of Honor,' and a 'Kennedy Centre Honor.'

He was also given the 'Presidential Medal of Freedom.' He earned the 'Golden Globe Cecil B. DeMille Award' in 2020. He is a humanist who has freely spoken his views on same-sex weddings. As an environmentalist, he recognizes the need for alternative fuels and has stated a willingness to contribute a substantial quantity of money to promote electric automobiles. His early goal of becoming an astronaut has turned him into a staunch supporter of NASA's manned space program.

 # Chapter 1

The Biography of Tom Hanks

On July 9, 1956, in Concord, California, Thomas Jeffrey Hanks, an American actor, was born. Hanks was reared by his father, Amos Mefford Hanks, an English cuisine chef, and his mother, Janet Marylyn, a nurse. He was reared with Catholic and Mormon religious ideals. He took theatrical school with his closest buddy at Skyline High School in Oakland. Hanks displayed his dramatic skill throughout his teens, winning the Best Theater Actor prize at his institution. Later, he enrolled in Chabot College in Hayward, California, then performed an exchange at California State University, Sacramento two years later.

When Reader's Digest surveyed in 2013 to determine the 100 Most Trusted People in America, Tom Hanks ranked first. It's no wonder that the adored hero of films like Big, Forrest Gump, Castaway, and Toy Story is one of Hollywood's most strong and well-respected performers. His approachability and charm have garnered him comparisons to film giants such as Jimmy Stewart, Cary Grant, and Gary Cooper.

Tom Hanks is the "everyman" whose depictions cause us to rethink our own moral decisions. We ponder about what we would--and have done--while watching him on film. "And that's why we all love you so much," Oprah remarked of Hanks in a 2001 interview. "We recognize ourselves in your characters."

Until 1980, when he dropped out of college and came to New York City, he spent his summers performing and working at the Great Lakes Shakespeare Festival in Ohio. That same year, Hanks was cast in the comedy Bosom Buddies as Kip Wilson, one of two advertising execs who dress in drag to rent an apartment in an all-female complex. The exposure led to cameo appearances on shows such as Happy Days, Taxi, The Love Boat, and Family Ties.

Ron Howard remembers Hanks from his appearance on Happy Days, and he cast him in Howard's 1984 blockbuster Splash with Daryl Hannah. Ron Howard and Tom

Hanks would later collaborate on Apollo 13, The Da Vinci Code, and Angels & Demons.

Penny Marshall hired Hanks in the star-making role of Big in 1988. His performance garnered him his first Academy Award nomination for Best Performer and cemented his status as both a box-office attraction and a great performer.

Hanks' performance with co-star Meg Ryan in Nora Ephron's 1993 classic Sleepless in Seattle cemented his position among the top romantic-comedy actors of his time. But it was his brave portrayal in Philadelphia as a lawyer sacked from his high-paying company because he had AIDS that earned him an Academy Award for Best Actor. Following the remarkable box office success of Forrest Gump in 1994, Hanks won his second consecutive Best Actor, Oscar, becoming just the second actor to do so after Spencer Tracy.

Hanks transitioned from in front of to behind the camera, making his directing and scripting debut with That Thing You Do! in 1996. Hanks produced, directed, wrote, and performed in many episodes of the Emmy-winning HBO miniseries From the Earth to the Moon. "I don't naturally excel at directing." Hanks said in a July 2014 interview that he learned how to do it from observing other individuals.

When he was featured in Steven Spielberg's gruesomely authentic World War II movie Saving Private Ryan, he formed an essential friendship with the director. The two developed Catch Me If You Can and The Terminal, as well as the miniseries Band of Brothers and its companion piece The Pacific, and the Cold War spy drama Bridge of Spies. During his AFI Life Achievement Award acceptance speech, Spielberg said of Hanks, "Tom Hanks' achievements in the film are many, but perhaps his greatest contribution so far is that he gives us all a lot of hope for a society where regular people have a voice.

Hanks has won various honors, including becoming the American Film Institute's Lifetime Achievement Award's youngest recipient. Hanks received a Tony Award nomination for his Broadway debut in Lucky Guy in 2013. His accomplishments, however, go beyond movies. Hanks received the Douglas S. Morrow Public Outreach Award from the Space Foundation, which is granted yearly to a someone or group that has made substantial contributions to public understanding of space projects. Hanks was the first actor to be admitted into the United States Army Rangers Hall of Fame as an honorary member. He served as the national spokesperson for the World War II Memorial Campaign as well as the honorary chairman of the D-Day Museum Capital Campaign.

Hanks' performances are indelible, whether he is experiencing a dramatic physical metamorphosis as in Castaway, playing a washed-up baseball icon turned manager in

A League of Their Own, or portraying Captain Phillips in real life.

Hanks said, "I'd like to think that somehow, even if it's in this big, false, glamorous arena of movies, I've reflected the audience's lives." "I hope people recognize themselves in some way on the screen." Shakespeare said, "Hold the mirror to nature." Human conduct is worth investigating and celebrating."

Chapter 2

A Look at Tom Hanks's Early Life and Career

In 1978, his portrayal as 'Proteus' in Shakespeare's 'The Two Gentlemen of Verona' earned him the Cleveland Critics Circle's Best Actor award.

From 1978 to 1980, he appeared in many summer performances of Shakespeare's plays and worked for a Sacramento theatrical group in the winter.

He went to New York in 1979 intending to play on Broadway. He made his film debut in the low-budget horror film 'He Knows You're Alone' in 1980.

He received critical recognition for his performance in the television comedy 'Bosom Buddies the same year.

His surprise appearance on the TV episode of 'Happy Days' in 1982 intrigued co-actor Ron Howard, who encouraged him to feature in the supporting role in 'Splash,' a comedic picture that became a huge blockbuster in 1984.

His portrayal in Penny Marshall's 'Big' (1988) as a 13-year-old child imprisoned in the body of a 35-year-old man was praised, and he quickly started starring in blockbuster successes.

His outstanding performance in the 1988 film 'Punchline' earned him a Los Angeles Film Critics Association Award.

His big break came in 1993 when he portrayed an AIDS-stricken attorney in Jonathan Demme's film "Philadelphia." He lost 37 pounds for the film and received an Oscar and an MTV Movie Award for his performance.

In 1994, he played the lead role in the movie 'Forrest Gump', an epic romantic-comedy-drama, based on the eponymous novel by Winston Groom. He received an Academy Award for his performance in the film.

In 1998, he collaborated with Steven Spielberg for the first time, playing a demanding part in 'Saving Private Ryan,' which earned him his fourth Academy Award nomination for Best Actor.

In 2001, he drew national prominence when he was cast in 'Band of Brothers,' an HBO mini-series, and 'A Tribute to Heroes,' both of which he directed.

In 2004, he was featured in many films, including The Ladykillers by the Coen Brothers, The Terminal by Steven Spielberg, and The Polar Express by Robert Zemeckis.

In 2006, he collaborated with Ron Howard to portray Robert Langdon in 'The Da Vinci

Code,' an adaptation of Dan Brown's book of the same name.

He co-produced 'The Great Buck Howard' (2008), in which his son Colin Hanks also appeared.

In 2009, he reprised his role as the legendary Robert Langdon in 'Angels and Demons,' a sequel to 'The Da Vinci Code,' which launched him to prominence.

He was an executive producer on the 2012 film 'Game Change,' which was based on the 2008 presidential campaign.

1981 - Making his acting debut

The Hanks family relocated to New York in 1979, giving Tom the chance to make his film debut as a supporting actor in the horror thriller "Sabe que estás sola" in 1981. He received a main part in another picture two years later. In addition, he made his television debut in the comedy series "Bosom Buddies." Later, he opted to go to Los Angeles to appear in "Despedida de Soltero" in 1984. Although the film was not a commercial success, it did enable him to be spotted by Ron Howard, who later contacted him to give him a role in "Splash" in 1984.

Tom has since appeared in other comedies, including "Amigos del alma" (1980), "Esta casa es una ruina" (1986), "Big" (1988), "No matarás... al vecino" (1989), "Socios y sabuesos" (1989), and "Joe contra el volcán" (1990). His father was always supportive of his work, urging him to keep striving for his ambition. He assisted him in obtaining minor parts on multiple occasions. He also encouraged him to attend the Great Lakes Shakespeare Festival in Cleveland, Ohio.

"The King of Comedy"

Following a brief appearance in Armand Mastroianni's horror film "He Knows You're Alone" (1980), he featured in many comedies that typecast him in humorous roles. His endearing demeanor and natural skill aided his rising popularity. His consecration occurred in the 1980s when he was dubbed the "King of Comedy." He received significant recognition with his portrayal in "Big" (1988), getting the Los Angeles Critics Award and an Oscar nomination. After that, he made a bit of a comeback as a disillusioned former baseball pitcher who coaches a women's team in "A League of Their Own" (1992).

Tom thought it was time to branch out and explore other tales, to get away from the humor for a while. As a result, he sought more dramatic topics in which he could demonstrate his flexibility. He sought to move away from light comedies with his work in "The Bonfire of the Vanities" (1989), directed by Brian de Palma, but the outcome was not as intended.

Some of his most well-known performances

Hanks rose to prominence as one of Hollywood's brightest stars in the mid-1990s. It's worth noting that his career was very successful. For his performance in

Robert Zemeckis' "Forrest Gump" (1994), one of the most memorable films of the decade, he was again worthy of an Oscar, a reward that rose, making him one of Hollywood's highest-paid performers. His first feature film was the comedic film "The Wonders" (1996).

Later, he accomplished the same in the production area with the TV series "From the Earth to the Moon," which took him many years to complete. Hanks played the lead in Steven Spielberg's feature film "Saving Private Ryan" (1997), for which he was nominated for an Academy Award. The film garnered five Oscars. In 2000, he collaborated once again with Robert Zemeckis on the film "Cast Away," for which his solo performance was lauded and earned him an Oscar nomination.

Between 2003 and 2004, he worked with Spielberg again on "Catch Me If You Can" and "The Terminal." In 2006, he appeared in "The Da Vinci Code," the film adaptation of Dan Brown's controversial bestseller. Hanks' movies have made over 4.2 billion in countries like the United States and Canada since 2014, and over 8.4 billion worldwide; he is unquestionably a performer who assures cinematic success. His celebrity is so widespread that the asteroid (12818) Tomhanks bears his name.

 # Chapter 3

Find out Tom Hanks Net Worth

Tom Hanks' net worth is reported to be approximately $400 million. This wealth has been amassed throughout his illustrious four-decade career as an actor, writer, director, and executive producer.

Hanks' success has allowed him to amass substantial wealth, which will no doubt expand with each new project he does.

Where did Tom Hanks get his money?
Tom Hanks has amassed a sizable wealth over the last several decades, owing mostly to his long-running film career. Let's look at how Tom Hanks earned his money.

1. Acting

Hanks' cinematic career started in 1980 with a small part in the horror thriller He Knows You're Alone. This led to more opportunities, including guest appearances on TV shows like Happy Days and Bosom Buddies. In the fantasy romantic comedy Splash, Hanks scored his first substantial starring role. His big break came with the 1988 smash film Big, for which he received his first Academy Award nomination.

Hanks has since appeared in several hit films, including Forrest Gump, Saving Private Ryan, Castaway, and The Terminal.

2. Endorsements

Tom Hanks has also earned money by promoting numerous items and businesses.

He has worked with companies such as Hanx Writer, Intel, Sony, and Starbucks.

3. Movies

In addition to That Thing You Do!, Castaway, My Big Fat Greek Wedding, and The Da Vinci Code, Hanks has produced and directed other films. He also formed the production business Playtone, which has worked on films including Charlie Wilson's War and Mamma Mia.

4. Investments

Tom Hanks also made savvy investments, such as paying $3.25 million for a beachfront home in Malibu Colony in 1991, which is now worth more than $20 million. In addition, in 2010, his principal house in Pacific Palisades was valued at $26 million.

He has also made real estate investments, which contribute to around $150 million of his net worth.

5. Public Speaking Engagements

Tom Hanks often gives speeches at gatherings and conferences. He charges a hefty speaking fee of more than $200,000 for every presentation. Personal appearances, such as book signings and corporate engagements, are also charged for by Hanks.

6. Music

Tom Hanks is also a musician who has published several CDs, including The Polar Express, Hot Chocolate, and others. Over the years, his music profession has provided him with extra cash.

7. Television

Tom Hanks has also enjoyed television success. He was an executive producer on the hit HBO series Band of Brothers and has been on The Simpsons and Saturday Night Live. In addition, he appeared in the miniseries From the Earth to the Moon and The Pacific.

Tom Hanks has increased his fortune by appearing on television and becoming a household celebrity. He continues to feature in television programs, cementing his reputation as one of the most known performers on television.

Tom Hanks has made millions of dollars from these and other television appearances during his career.

8. Merchandising

With his enormous popularity, it is unsurprising that Tom Hanks has generated money selling merchandise. He has created various lines of high-quality products based on some of his most famous performances and films.

From Big-inspired T-shirts to Castaway popcorn buckets and eye-catching posters, this memorabilia is available from independent artists in shops and online. Tom Hanks' merchandise includes items from his earlier films, like Forrest Gump, Apollo 13, and Saving Private Ryan.

The high quality of the stuff has made it highly popular among Tom Hanks's followers, guaranteeing that merchandising accounts for a major portion of his riches.

9. Books

Tom Hanks has published two books, one of which is a collection of short stories called Uncommon Type. For children, he authored The Purple Burrito of Oz and its sequel, The Amazing Adventures of Captain Marvelous.

These novels have been very successful, providing Tom Hanks with extra income and increasing his net worth. Tom Hanks has amassed millions of dollars through his many businesses throughout his career, making him one of Hollywood's richest performers.

He is a well-liked actor who is still participating in several projects that earn him fortune and renown. His success can only be sustained if he continues to seek out fresh chances.

Chapter 4

Tom's Marriages and his Children: All You Need to Know

Throughout his life, the actor has been married multiple times. In 1978, he married Samantha Lewes, with whom he had two children: Colin Hanks in 1977 and Elisabeth Ann in 1982. The couple split in 1985, though. He then married actress and producer Rita Wilson in 1988, with whom he had two more children: Chester Marlon in 1991 and Truman Theodore in 1996. The actor has just been diagnosed with type 2 diabetes, which requires a precise diet and daily care to keep him healthy.

Tom Hanks and his first wife Samantha divorced despite having children together; she died 15 years later.

The media often refers to actor Tom Hanks and his longtime wife, Rita Wilson, as a marriage made in heaven. However, nothing is known about Hanks' first wife, Samantha Lewes, who died when he was young.

Hanks was previously married to Samantha Lewes. Unfortunately, their marriage only lasted nine years until they divorced in 1987.

Few facts about the late actress:

1. **Lewes was a performer**

Lewes, who was born Susan Jane Dillingham on November 29, 1952, rose to recognition as an actor in the 1980s. She appeared in the successful movies "Mr. Success" in 1980 and "Bosom Buddies" in 1984.

Although her educational background was never made public, it is assumed that Lewes was well-educated and had a love for acting at an early age.

2. Lewes and Hanks attended same school

Her connection with Hanks was the most intimate aspect of her life that anybody knew about. According to stories, Lewes and Hanks originally met while studying acting at Sacramento State University.

They were merely friends at the moment, but their friendship rapidly developed into something more serious. By 1978, the young actors had chosen to marry.

3. Lewes and Hanks wedding

Hanks was just 23 when they married, while Lewes was 27. The age gap didn't matter to them, and the public saw them as the ideal pair throughout their time together.

The couple has two children: Colin, born in 1977, and Elizabeth, born in 1982. Everything was going well for the couple until 1984 when they decided to start living in separate houses.

4. The Cause of Their Divorce

Initially, it was assumed that the pair fell apart owing to misunderstandings and issues, which led to their divorce in 1987.

However, Hanks once acknowledged that this was not the case.

The actor revealed that he married too young and afterward realized that it was not the best decision to make at that age. He went on to say that he wasn't ready to take on the burden of raising a kid at the moment.

5. Concerning his Children

Growing up in a fractured household, the "Forrest Gump" star didn't want his children to go through the same thing. However, he felt compelled to take action.

Even though he had no vices, Hanks stated that he might have been a far better father back then. Being better means being there for them, explaining things more thoroughly, and not being too busy with other matters.

6. Hanks discussing their divorce

Divorce was a painful choice for both Lewes and Hanks, but it was one they had to make. In 2013, he spoke out about it, saying:

"A broken marriage meant I was condemning my children to the same feelings I had when they were their age." I was just too young and insecure to marry."

7. Colin's Profession

Colin and Elizabeth are both actors, according to their children. Colin, on the other hand, seems to be more busy, since he is also a producer and director.

He is well recognized for his roles in "Orange County," "King Kong," "The House Bunny," and the "Jumanji" film series, as well as several significant television appearances.

8. Elizabeth's Profession

Meanwhile, Elizabeth is known for her roles in "Forrest Gump," a 1994 American comedy-drama, "That Thing You Do!" a comedic musical from 1996, and the short drama "Anchorage."

Elizabeth is also a writer and an influential person in the American publishing scene, and she presently works as the Children's Editor for the Los Angeles Review of Books.

9. Lewes' Cancer Fight

Following her divorce from Hanks, Lewes maintained a quiet profile while caring for their children. She was eventually diagnosed with bone cancer, which she battled for the remainder of her life.

According to accounts, the news crushed the "The Terminal" star. Despite their ups and downs throughout the years, they remained friends.

10. Her Death in 2002

Lewes died on March 12, 2002, at her home in Carmichael, Sacramento County, California. At the time, she was 49 years old. She was put to rest at the nearby East Lawn Memorial Park, and Hanks grieved with his two children. He had the finest support system in his second wife Rita Wilson throughout it all.

Chapter 5

Tom Hanks Second Marriage

Hanks is now well-known for his lengthy marriage to Wilson. They've been married for nearly three decades, and it all started in 1984 on the set of "Volunteers."

Wilson's charisma drew Hanks in. Even their co-stars could tell at the time that they were "fond of each other." It was just a matter of time until they met.

Relationship of Tom Hanks and Rita Wilson Everlasting love! For decades, Tom Hanks and Rita Wilson have shown that Hollywood romances can withstand the test of time.

When it came to his ultimate marriage, according to the Cast Away star, it was love at first sight — even though he didn't meet her until years later.

The California native fell in love with Wilson when she made her television debut as Pat Conway on The Brady Bunch in 1972. "Oh, I just watch it on YouTube now and then." "Everything she was in," Hanks told The Knot and other reporters in 2016. "I was at a friend's house at the time, and I remember thinking, 'That girl is cute.'"

Sparks flew between the two as soon as they met on the set of Bosom Buddies in 1981. At the time, Samantha Lewes, his college girlfriend, and Hanks were wed.

When the two met for Volunteers in 1984, their connection was unmistakable, and the two began dating — after the Splash actor's marriage ended a few years later. Although his divorce was not completed until 1987, Hanks and Wilson began dating in 1986.

The couple married on April 30, 1988, and Wilson's short wedding gown is still spoken about by admirers.

They've always bragged about one other and supported each other's professions throughout their partnership. They have traveled together for movie productions and the Jingle All the Way actress' singing career.

Wilson explains the secret to the couple's marital happiness in April 2019.

The Runaway Bride actress said that she and her husband "got married, committed to each other, love each other, and work hard on our relationship." "Not only do we love each other, but we also really like each other, and we enjoy being together, and we support each other and keep the lines of communication open." That is always essential."

The Marriage Journey of Hanks and Rita

In December 1981

In 1981, the pair met on the set of Bosom Buddies. Hanks was a regular on the ABC sitcom, portraying Kip Wilson and Buffy Wilson, while his future wife guest-starred on the "All You Need Is Love" episode, which aired on December 18, 1981.

1984

The performers reunited in 1984 for the 1985 film Volunteers. Lawrence (Hanks), a Yale graduate and womanizer, goes to the peace corps because his father refuses to pay off his gambling problem. While in Thailand, he meets Tacoma residents Tom Tuttle (John Candy) and Beth Wexler (Wilson). The picture sparked a relationship between the actors, which rapidly blossomed into romance.

March 1987

Following their first public appearance as a couple at the Three Amigos premiere in December 1986, the pair attended the 1987 Academy Awards, launching their reign as one of Hollywood's favorite power couples.

1988

The couple married in 1988, and Hanks is still certain he found the correct match. "There was a kind of (pointing to camera) 'Hey, this is the place!' when we exchanged our initial glances. Regarding his marriage to Wilson, he admitted to Entertainment Tonight in 2015, "I felt that anyway." We got married for all the right reasons, I believe, as a result.

The month of January 1989

At the 1989 Golden Globes, Hanks expressed his gratitude to his new spouse. "I married a Greek babe," he joked after accepting the Best Actor award for Big. "She was born in California, in Hollywood, but her parents are wonderful, and she's wonderful, Rita Wilson—thank you, babe, for marrying me." You've already made my year, but thank you.

August of 1990

On August 4, 1990, the newlywed couple had their first child, son Chester, also known as Chet.

June 1992

Wilson was there when the Sully star earned his star on the Hollywood Walk of Fame in June 1992.

The year 1993

The couple reunited in 1992 for the 1993 picture Sleepless in Seattle. Wilson portrayed Suzy, Hanks' character Sam's closest buddy, in the film. Sam finds love with Meg Ryan's Annie with the assistance of Suzy and a radio talk program.

March 1995

The California native earned an Academy Award for Best Actor for Philadelphia and Forrest Gump in 1994 and 1995, respectively. Throughout both remarks, the actor thanked his wife for her unwavering support. In 1995, he said, "I am here because the woman I share my life with teaches me and proves to me every day what love is."

In December of 1995,

Truman Theodore, the couple's second child, was born on December 26, 1995. They had been to London a few months before to see Princess Diana at the premiere of Apollo 13.

The year 2002

In 2002, they collaborated on their first production endeavor, My Big Fat Greek Wedding. In 2016, they released the sequel, My Big Fat Greek Wedding 2, as well as Mamma Mia! and in addition to Mamma Mia! Here We Go Again.

May 2012

Wilson remarked on one of her many romantic moments with her spouse when appearing on Piers Morgan Tonight in May 2012. "I'll never forget, we were standing on the corner of 57th and 5th in New York, or 58th and 5th," the Now and Then star recounted. "We were holding hands as we waited for the light to change." And he looked at me and said, 'You know, I just want you to know that you never have to alter anything about who you are to be with me.'" She said, "If love is a sensation or a molecular thing that occurs to your body, it literally went through me, and that's pretty much who he is, and how he's been.

April 2015

The Jingle All the Way actress revealed in April 2015 that she had been diagnosed with breast cancer. Her spouse stayed at her side throughout her battle with the sickness.

"Who knew it would bring you closer together?" In May 2015, Wilson informed The New York Times about how the sickness affected her relationship with Hanks. "In situations like this, you never know how your spouse will react." My husband's compassion for me amazed me over and again. It was such a typical, private moment."

In October of 2016

The pair explained that they travel extensively for their various projects, such as Italy for Hanks' film Inferno or all around the United States for Wilson's self-titled record. "We're having so much fun. Being on site is one of the finest aspects, Wilson narrated in October 2016. "We've traveled all over the world." We've brought our whole family. We've gotten to live in cities where you wouldn't typically be able to reside and become regular people, going to the market and choosing your favorite coffee shop and shop. You're just pretending to be a native, which is fantastic. You're not in a hurry."

March 2019

On March 30, 2019, the Broadway actress earned a star on the Hollywood Walk of Fame. Of course, her spouse of over 30 years was there to brag about her and her achievements. "She has a highlight reel that any of us would envy," Hanks stated during the award presentation. She had been featured in publications, TV programs, and advertisements thanks to her smile and charisma, but there was still more for her to accomplish and learn with her heart and head.

April 2019

The It's Complicated actress shared with Us Weekly exclusively in April 2019 how her friendship with the Oscar winner has changed over the previous three decades. "It's just like anything," Wilson said. "We married, committed to each other, love each other, and work hard to maintain our relationship." We not only love one another, but we also like each other. We like being together, we support each other, and we keep the lines of communication open. That is always essential."

The month of January 2020

The 77th annual Golden Globe Awards presented the Cecil B. DeMille Award to the star of A Man Called Ove in January 2020. Hanks lavished love on his family throughout his address, which drew a standing ovation. I am a fortunate guy. He sobbed, "I'm blessed to have a family like that sitting up front." "A wonderful wife who has shown me what love is all about." Five children who are more resilient, intelligent, and strong than their father, as well as a supportive family that has put up with my extended absences. He went on to say, "I can't tell you how much your love means to me."

March 2020

On March 11, 2020, the Band of Brothers producer said that he and his wife tested positive for the coronavirus while in Australia filming an unnamed Elvis Presley biopic. "Hello, folks," Hanks wrote back then. "Rita and I are now in Australia. We felt fatigued, as if we had colds, and our bodies ached. Rita had intermittent chills. There was also a little temperature. We were tested for the coronavirus and found to be positive, which is how things must be done in the modern world.

He updated his fans the next day, citing his 1992 picture A League of Their Own. "Aren't there things we can all do to help each other and ourselves get through this by listening to experts and taking care of ourselves?"

Hanks shared on Instagram. "Remember, no crying in baseball, regardless of current events."

April 2020

Wilson talked out about being together in sickness and in health after the couple's recovery from COVID-19 in late March. According to the singer, "I think having the virus at the same time made it that little bit easier," she said in an interview with The Guardian on April 17. "We were taking care of each other instead of having the pressure of caring for one person and no one caring for you or understanding that the person at home needs a break."

April 2020

Before their 32nd anniversary in April, the Sleepless in Seattle actress raved over her spouse, reminiscing on what originally attracted her to Hanks. "We just got along instantly," Wilson remarked on The Kelly Clarkson Show in April. "First and foremost, I like good storytelling. So I'm down with anybody who can tell a good narrative."

The fact that the Oscar winner was highly talkative when they first met clinched the deal for the singer, which blended in well with her "very vocal" Greek family. "Talking and food were pretty much our entire existence," she went on. "I adore that. He never fails to make me chuckle. He's a fantastic storyteller."

April 2020

On April 30, the pair celebrated their one-month anniversary after returning to Los Angeles after the couple's COVID-19 struggle and recovery. "I've known this man for 32 years! @tomhanks "Happy Anniversary, my love," Wilson said on Instagram to commemorate the occasion. "Let's go 32 more times and then some!"

"33 years of marriage to my best lover, friend, and man." Love wins out. Wilson poured her heart out to her spouse on their wedding anniversary.

July 2021

"I'm riding into 65 stronger than ever!" Happy birthday to my life's love! "Xox,"

Wilson said on Instagram to commemorate her husband's birthday on July 9.

June 2022

Hanks protected his wife on a New York City trip when a swarm of admirers almost knocked her down. "What about my wife?" Back the f-ck up! "Knocking over my wife?" the Elvis impersonator asked the audience before getting into a vehicle with Wilson.

Wilson tweeted a photo of her husband looking peaceful in the woods on his 66th birthday in July 2022. "Congratulations on your birthday!" I adore you and think about you every day. She posted on Instagram.

February 20, 2023

At Clive Davis' traditional pre-Grammys event, the married pair matched in black.

In March 2023, President Joe Biden welcomed the A Man Called Otto actor and country singer to the White House to commemorate Greek Independence Day.

April 2023

On April 30, 2023, the pair celebrated their 35th wedding anniversary. "It's been 35 years of marriage. April 30, 1988. "Love is everything," Wilson captioned an Instagram snap of Hanks holding up a cake with the words "Happy Anniversary."

Where does Tom Hanks call home?

Tom Hanks and his wife Rita Wilson reside in the Pacific Palisades district of Los Angeles.

What is the cost of Tom Hanks' home?

The couple paid $26 million for Tom Hanks' Pacific Palisades house in 2010, but the price has subsequently increased to $28.5 million.

Tom Hanks 's Siblings and What They Do.

Tom Hanks' family consists of three siblings: Sandra Hanks, Larry Hanks, and Jim Hanks. Larry teaches entomology at the University of Illinois in Urbana-Champaign, in opposition to Sandra.

Jim Hanks, Tom Hanks' younger brother, is also an actor who contributed to a number of Tom's most well-known roles. Even if Jim Hanks hasn't attained the same level of celebrity as his brother, chances are you've seen or heard some of his live-action or voiceover work during his decades-long career in cinema and television.

Jim Hanks is the youngest of four children, the result of a divorce between his parents, Amos and Janet, while he was a youngster. Following the couple's divorce, Janet transferred her youngest boy to the city of Red Bluff in the state of California, while Amos relocated the three elder children to various locales around Northern California.

Chapter 6

Hanks Personal Life

6.1. Hanks' Role as a Veteran and Military Family Advocate

Tom Hanks is not just a superb actor; he is also an outspoken supporter of soldiers and their families. He has utilized his position and influence to raise awareness of the difficulties that these people face. He has worked valiantly to assist them in a variety of ways.

Hanks' engagement with the military started with his role in the film "Saving Private Ryan." A World War II epic depicting American troops' sacrifices and courage.

The film was a financial and critical triumph, and Hanks was nominated for an Academy Award for Best Actor. His involvement with the military community, however, did not cease with the publication of the film.

Hanks produced and narrated the documentary "We Stand Alone Together" in 2003. In addition, "The Men of Easy Company" recorded the experiences of troops who served in the 101st Airborne Division during WWII. The documentary was developed in conjunction with the HBO miniseries "Band of Brothers," which Hanks also executive produced.

Hanks has been a prominent champion for soldiers and military families in addition to his job in the entertainment business. He has collaborated with groups such as the USO and the Elizabeth Dole Foundation to assist veterans and their families.

He has also utilized his public platform to raise awareness about the challenges that these people face. They include PTSD, severe brain damage, and the difficulties of returning to civilian life.

6.2. Contributions of Tom Hanks to the Worlds of Podcasting and Audio Entertainment

Aside from performing, Hanks has made substantial contributions to podcasting and audio entertainment.

Hanks has always been a devotee of old-time radio plays. His love of the media inspired him to start a podcast called "The Hanx Writer's Room."

Hanks and his colleagues explore the craft of storytelling and their appreciation of old typewriters in the podcast. Hanks also tells his unique tales. He offered comments on historic radio plays as well as the works of authors such as Ernest Hemingway and F. Scott Fitzgerald.

In addition to "The Hanx Writer's Room," Hanks has provided narration for several other audio works. He narrated Stephen Ambrose's audiobook, "Band of Brothers."

The book relates the narrative of Easy Company troops during World War II. Hanks' narration brings the book's characters and events to life, and his performance demonstrates his storytelling prowess.

Hanks has collaborated with the podcast network Wondery on a limited series titled "The Outpost." It relates the tale of the United States Army's most dangerous outpost in Afghanistan.

The series is based on Jake Tapper's book and stars a cast of actors, including Hanks, representing troops and civilians who lived and worked at the outpost.

6.3. Hanks' media image and public relations

Hanks' Opinions on Storytelling and the Role of Entertainment in Society

The celebrated actor and director Tom Hanks has talked widely about the value of narrative and the role of entertainment in society. Storytelling, according to Hanks, is important to the human experience. It has the capacity, he believes, to influence our perspective of the world around us.

Hanks has said that he is a "storyteller by nature." He views storytelling as a means of connecting individuals from different cultures and generations. He thinks that tales may bridge the gap between diverse groups by helping us comprehend the lives and viewpoints of others.

According to Hanks, entertainment may be used to educate and enlighten people as well as amuse them. He has often stated his conviction that films, television programs, and other forms of entertainment can be utilized to investigate serious societal problems and stimulate meaningful dialogue.

Hanks has also stressed the significance of honesty and sincerity in storytelling. He thinks that excellent storytelling requires a dedication to authenticity and candor. Storytellers, according to him, have a duty to depict the world in a manner that is both true and courteous.

6.4. Hanks' Environmental Advocacy and Climate Change Action

Tom Hanks is not just a well-known actor, director, and producer, but also an outspoken supporter of environmental concerns and climate change action. Throughout his career, he has utilized his position to raise awareness about the significance of environmental protection and climate change action.

Advocacy

Throughout his career, Tom Hanks has been active in a variety of environmental advocacy projects. He has served on the National Space Society's board of directors and as a trustee of the Natural Resources Defense Council. He has also worked to promote environmental education and sustainability.

In 2011, Hanks narrated the documentary film "The Arctic Light," which focused on the beauty of the Arctic as well as the effects of climate change on the area. He has also participated in initiatives to promote renewable energy and lower carbon emissions.

Climate Change Intervention

Tom Hanks has been an outspoken supporter of climate change action. He signed an open letter from the entertainment sector in 2015 pushing world leaders to negotiate a strong climate accord at the United Nations Climate Change Conference in Paris. He has also spoken out on the need of lowering carbon emissions and shifting to renewable energy sources.

In 2017, Hanks appeared in the documentary film "Before the Flood," which investigated the environmental consequences of climate change and the necessity for rapid action to solve the problem. He has also taken part in projects to encourage electric cars and minimize plastic waste.

6.5. Hank's political involvement

Throughout his career, Tom Hanks has been an active participant in political action. Using his notoriety to advocate for issues and encourage political participation.

Supporting political candidates and ideas, speaking out on significant political problems, and participating in political campaigns and events have all been part of his political involvement.

Supporting political candidates and causes has been a focal point of Hanks' political engagement. He has been an outspoken supporter and donor to Democratic politicians such as Barack Obama and Hillary Clinton.

Hanks has also participated in Democratic Party fundraising events and pushed for the party's policy on subjects such as climate change, education, and healthcare.

Hanks has also taken a stand on significant political topics. Hanks has also been an advocate for women's rights, speaking out against gender inequity and employment discrimination.

Hanks has engaged in political campaigns and events in addition to supporting political candidates and topics. He has engaged in voter registration drives and get-out-the-vote activities during elections.

Hanks has also taken part in political rallies and marches, leveraging his fame to call attention to vital causes and inspire political participation.

6.6 Acts of philanthropy and social responsibility

Tom Hanks is well-known for his charitable work and sense of social responsibility. He has been engaged in several activities aimed at supporting significant causes and bettering the lives of people and communities all around the globe.

Donations to charity organizations, support for different causes, and engagement in social responsibility projects have all been part of his philanthropic efforts.

One of Hanks' primary charitable initiatives has been to promote education. He has given millions of dollars to educational institutions, notably California State University, Sacramento, his alma school.

Hanks has also been an outspoken supporter of educational reform. He has also backed programs to expand educational access for pupils from underprivileged neighborhoods.

Hanks has also participated in efforts encouraging healthy living and exercise, such as his support for the Los Angeles Marathon.

Hanks has also been involved in assisting soldiers and their families. He has been active in several programs that give assistance and services to veterans, such as the "Honour. Learn. Remember" campaign.

Its goal was to inform the public about the sacrifices made by veterans. Hanks has also donated to groups that help veterans and their families with healthcare, housing, and other needs.

 # Chapter 7

Tom's Collaborations and sponsorships

Tom Hanks is a well-known actor, director, and producer who has worked with several businesses and musicians over his career. Collaborations and sponsorships have allowed him to broaden his influence, grow his fan base, and support vital causes.

Collaborations

On different projects, Tom Hanks has collaborated with several renowned actors and directors. Among his most prominent partnerships are:

Steven Spielberg: Tom Hanks has collaborated on multiple projects with Steven Spielberg, including "Saving Private Ryan," "Catch Me If You Can," and "Bridge of Spies."

Tom Hanks has also worked with director Robert Zemeckis on multiple films, including "Forrest Gump," "Cast Away," and "The Polar Express."

Tom Hanks collaborated with Paul Greengrass on the 2013 picture "Captain Phillips."

Tom Hanks has collaborated with Ron Howard on various projects, including "Apollo 13," "The Da Vinci Code," and "Angels & Demons."

Emma Watson: Tom Hanks and Emma Watson collaborated on the 2017 picture "The Circle."

Tom Hanks has also worked on sponsorships with many products and enterprises. Among his famous sponsorships are:

AT&T: Tom Hanks appeared in a series of AT&T advertisements in 2016 to promote the company's cellular service and DirecTV.

IBM: Since 2016, Tom Hanks has served as an IBM brand ambassador, supporting the company's Watson AI technology.

Tom Hanks has long been a supporter of the National Park Foundation, acting as the spokesman for the organization's "Find Your Park" campaign.

Toyota: Tom Hanks appeared in a Toyota ad in 2016 promoting the company's Mirai fuel cell car.

Chapter 8

The Legacy of Tom Hanks as an Actor, Producer, and Humanitarian

---

Throughout his distinguished career, Tom Hanks has left a great legacy as an actor, producer, and philanthropist. Not only has he given some of the most unforgettable performances in film history, but he has also utilized his platform to promote awareness and support for different humanitarian issues.

Actor's Legacies

Tom Hanks is largely recognized as one of the finest performers of all time, with a career spanning many decades and including countless memorable performances. He has a great range and variety as an actor, effortlessly shifting between humorous and tragic parts.

Hanks has received several prizes and honors for his ability and services to the film business.

His performances in films such as "Forrest Gump," "Philadelphia," and "Cast Away" have become part of movie history, inspiring and resonating with viewers even now.

Producer's Legacy

Tom Hanks has had a big effect on the film business as a producer in addition to his starring career. With his producing partner

Gary Goetzman, he formed Play Tone and has produced several hit films and television programs.

Hanks' production firm has worked on highly acclaimed and award-winning films including "Band of Brothers," "The Pacific," and "John Adams."

Hanks' work as a producer has helped bring significant tales to the screen while also providing chances for other brilliant people in the business.

Humanitarian Legacies

Tom Hanks has also utilized his position to advocate for and generate funds for several humanitarian issues. He has worked to help veterans, promote education, and fight illnesses such as HIV/AIDS and cancer.

Hanks has contributed to some charities and causes, including the Elizabeth Glaser Paediatric AIDS Foundation, the Leukaemia & Lymphoma Society, and the Gary Sinise Foundation.

He has also been active in educational activities, sitting on the board of the California State University Foundation and giving to a variety of educational organizations.

 # Chapter 9

Tom Hanks' Personal Honors and Awards

Tom Hanks has earned several accolades and personal honors for his services to the film business and humanitarian activities during his successful career.

His brilliance, flexibility, and dedication to his profession have won him a position among the greatest performers of all time, and his charitable work has had a tremendous global influence.

1. Academic and business recognition

Tom Hanks has received various accolades and honors for his services to the film business. He has won two Academy Awards for Best Actor for his roles in "Philadelphia" and "Forrest Gump," and he has been nominated for countless other awards during his career.

Hanks has also received four Golden Globe Awards. He has received a Screen Actors Guild Award, a Primetime Emmy Award, and a Tony Award nomination for his Broadway performance.

He has a Hollywood Walk of Fame star and has been admitted into the American Academy of Arts and Sciences.

2. Humanitarian Honors and Awards

Tom Hanks has been acknowledged for his humanitarian activities in addition to his successes in the film business.

Hanks was awarded the Presidential Medal of Freedom. It is America's highest civilian honor, given in appreciation of his contributions to the arts and charity endeavors. In addition, he has received the Kennedy Center Honors, the French Legion of Honor, and the Order of the British Empire.

3. Personal Recognition

Throughout his career, Tom Hanks has won several personal honors. He received the American Film Institute Life Achievement Award in 2002 and was named one of Time magazine's "100 Most Influential People" in 2004.

In 2016, President Barack Obama presented Hanks with the Presidential Medal of Freedom. He was lauded by the president for his "powerful, honest portrayals of ordinary people in extraordinary circumstances."

Hanks has also been recognized for his services to the arts and culture by the Museum of Modern Art and the National Archives Foundation.

Chapter 10

Controversies and Setbacks: All You Need To Know

Tom Hanks has a generally excellent reputation. However, he has had his fair share of scandals and disappointments during his career, just like any other public personality.

1. One of Hanks' most public issues happened in 2018 when he was accused of complicity in Harvey Weinstein's alleged sexual assault.

Rose McGowan, an actress, accused Hanks of knowing about Weinstein's behavior but doing nothing. Hanks disputed the charges, claiming he was unaware of Weinstein's behavior. On the set of any of his films, he had never seen anything untoward.

2. Another incident concerning Hanks happened in 2019 when he was chastised for his performance in the film "A Beautiful Day in the Neighbourhood."

The film was criticized for being unduly sanitized and for not truly reflecting the life of Mr. Rogers, who was played by Tom Hanks in the film. Some critics also accused Hanks of using the position to boost his image as a wholesome and well-liked star.

Aside from these scandals, Hanks has faced obstacles in his career. One of the most prominent disappointments was when he produced and acted in the film "Larry Crowne" in 2011. The picture garnered poor reviews and was a commercial flop, costing Hanks and his production firm money.

Hanks has also had personal difficulties. His first marriage to Samantha Lewes ended in divorce in 1987. Hanks has talked openly about the effect Lewes' loss had on him and his family after she died from cancer in 2002.

Tom Hanks commercial endeavors

Tom Hanks is not only a renowned actor and producer, but he has also had a few remarkable business enterprises.

Hanks co-founded Playtone, a production firm responsible for numerous great films and television series, in 1993. Early works by the group included "That Thing You Do!" (1996) and Both "From the Earth to the Moon" (1998) and it were well reviewed by critics. More contemporary blockbusters, such as "Game Change" (2012) and "The Pacific" (2010), have also been generated using play tone.

Hanks has worked in the hotel business as well. In 2006, he joined forces with five other investors to acquire Hollywood's iconic Argyle Hotel.

The hotel was eventually refurbished and reopened as The Rebury, a boutique hotel.

Since then, the hotel has been a famous destination for both visitors and celebrities.

Hanks has been active in the technology business in addition to his production firm and hotel endeavors. In 2015, he invested in The Virtual Reality startup, a startup that specialized in creating high-quality virtual reality experiences.

Hanks has been an outspoken supporter of virtual reality, claiming that technology has the potential to transform the way we experience entertainment.

Hank's ambitious ambitions for the future
Tom Hanks has not publicly discussed any particular intentions for the future, but he has been engaged in several initiatives and

projects that reflect his interest in the future and desire to make a good difference.

Hanks is interested in the realm of virtual reality. He has been a proponent of the technology and has invested in The Virtual Reality Company. The firm uses virtual reality to create immersive experiences.

Hanks believes that virtual reality has the potential to revolutionize the way we experience entertainment and interact with our surroundings.

Hanks has also been active in many environmental efforts, demonstrating his concern for the planet's future. He has donated to the Nature Conservancy. It is a non-profit organization dedicated to the protection of natural resources.

Hanks has also participated in some projects aimed at lowering carbon emissions and boosting sustainability. It also includes carrying out a scheme to employ renewable energy sources to replace the energy used in Hollywood film and television production.

Hanks has also participated in programs to promote literacy and reading. He chaired the program for the National Ambassador for Young People's Literature.

Tom Hanks' 3 Success Lessons

Now that you know all there is to know about Tom Hanks' net worth and how he reached success, let's look at some of the lessons we can take from him:

1. Discover Love

You will discover love now and then, and occasionally that love will fade. Allow yourself to sink into self-pity or feel unlovable. You will fall in love again; keep an eye out for such occasions. establish an effort to establish new friends and locate a partner.

2. Never Give Up Hope

There is hope, even in the most dire situations. There is always something positive to be discovered in a difficult circumstance. Look for the good instead of the bad, and you'll discover that life's obstacles will become simpler to manage.

3. Speak Up for Yourself

Because life isn't always fair, you must advocate for yourself. Nobody can afford to be powerless, so don't allow others to use you. Learn to be tenacious, grab every chance, and pursue your goals.

Chapter 11

These are the 27 best Tom Hanks movies of all time

Tom Hanks has become a cultural icon after starring in countless masterpieces that grabbed our imaginations. He is the most popular movie actor of our time and is universally considered one of the very nicest people in Hollywood, both onstage and off.

President Barack Obama said it best when he presented Hanks with the Presidential Medal of Freedom: "He has introduced us to America's unassuming heroes." He has enabled us to view ourselves not just as we are, but also as we want to be."

Here is a list of the top Tom Hanks films of all time:

The Greatest Tom Hanks Films of All Time

1. The Burbs (1989).

By 1989, Hanks had become so famous with fans that despite negative reviews, The Burbs launched at the top of the box office due to his likability and star power. Bruce Dern, Carrie Fisher, Corey Feldman, and Rick Ducommon co-star in Joe Dante's The Burbs, which was released five years after his handcrafted mayhem Gremlins. It's about neighbors who fear the new residents are members of a violent cult. The Burbs, like past Dante ventures, employ innovative and eye-popping visual effects, but Hanks' breezily humorous presence is the most effective impact in an inconsistent picture.

2. Greyhound (2020).

At the height of the epidemic, two Hank films were published on Netflix to good reviews: News of the World on Netflix and Greyhound on Apple. Greyhound is directed by Aaron Schneider and co-stars Elizabeth Shue, Stephen Graham, and Hanks' son Chet Hanks. It's a low-fi World War II nautical thriller that fleshes out characters and stages thrilling action in 91 minutes, which is no small achievement. Greyhound was nominated for an Academy Award for Best Sound.

3. Sully, also known as Sully: Miracle on the Hudson (2016)

Hanks collaborated with filmmaker Clint Eastwood in this biopic/legal drama hybrid on Chesley "Sully" Sullenberger, which also starred Aaron Eckhart, Laura Linney, and Anna Gunn. Sully investigates the emergency landing of US Airways Flight 1549 on the Hudson River and the subsequent judicial probe. Sully lacks the weight of the director's or star's best work, but the set piece is captivating, as are the performers.

4. The World's News (2020)

Years after the huge success of Captain Phillips, Hanks, and director Paul Greengrass reunited for News of the World. The action thriller, based on the book of the same name, stars Hanks as a Civil War warrior who meets a 10-year-old girl (Helena Zengel) reared by Kiowa and goes over treacherous Texas territory to return her to her family. The pace of News of the World is perfect for a traditional Western: slow and explorative generally, yet nail-bitingly stressful at points.

5. Turner and Hooch (1989)

Turner and Hooch are Tom Hanks and a large dog. Is there anything more high-concept enticing than that? Tomorrow Never Dies director Roger Spottiswoode directs the Oscar winner in a comic criminal caper about a strict investigator who inherits the Dogue de Bordeaux of a dead comrade. In 2021, the film will be converted into a Disney+ series. Be warned: this is a comedy that may need the use of a box of Kleenex.

6. A Lovely Day in the Neighborhood (2018)

Tom Hanks as Fred Rogers has to be one of the best casting choices ever. In Marielle Heller's drama A Beautiful Day in the Neighborhood, Hanks portrayed the adored, legendary children's television presenter. The Oscar-nominated film, written by Noah Harps and Micah Fitzerman-Blue, is based on the true story of real-life journalist Tom Junod (played by The American Emmy winner Matthew Rhys), whose life was transformed by the chance to interview Rogers for Esquire.

Hanks is flawless, and the film would have benefitted from more of his presence. It's a polite and even informative biography, but it should have been a home run with this ensemble.

7. Bridge of Spies (2015 film)

Hanks portrays real-life lawyer James B. Donovan in Steven Spielberg's Cold War-set Bridge of Spies, who is charged with a prisoner swap after defending a convicted KGB spy. Bridge of Spies, divided into two different sections, is light on its feet, a touch creaky at times, and largely satisfying—a notch below top-tier Spielberg.

Mark Rylance, who won Best Supporting Actor at the Oscars against favored Sylvester Stallone (Creed), outshines everyone in

Bridge of Spies. It was the night's greatest upset.

8. Joe Versus the Volcano (1990).

Before Sleepless in Seattle and You've Got Mail, Meg Ryan and Tom Hanks shone in Moonstruck, writer/director John Patrick Shanley's cult classic, underrated rom-com about a hypochondriac who appears to be dying and deciding to accept a billionaire eccentric's (Lloyd Bridges) offer to pass away peacefully in a secluded tropical volcano.

Ryan plays three characters in this unabashedly absurdist and mainly enjoyable comedy. Watching it all these years later, it's natural to hope that Hanks and Ryan would share the screen again.

9. (1996) That Thing You Do!

Hanks' directorial debut is an ensemble dramedy about a fictitious rock band a la The Beatles. High-energy That Thing You Do! is bright and enjoyable; it succeeds well in portraying a bygone age, and it's fluffier than other of Hanks' more innovative films from the 1990s. That's a high standard! A deleted sequence introduced Hanks, who portrays the band's homosexual manager, to NFL star Howie Long as his lover. Rita Wilson, Hanks' wife, also appears in the scene. It's rather amusing, and it's a pity it didn't make the final edit. Fortunately, it may now be seen in its entirety online.

10. You've Got Mail, 1998

The Shop Around the Corner, Nora Ephron's follow-up to Sleepless in Seattle, is a higher-tech ('90s!) replica of Ernst Lubitsch's classic. You've Got Mail, reuniting Ryan and Hanks as bitter business competitors who are secretly in love through dial-up, was a tremendous box-office triumph, generating over $250 million, greater than When Harry Met Sally or Sleepless in Seattle.

11. The Post (2017).

Steven Spielberg thought Liz Hannah's screenplay for this dramatic thriller about Katharine Graham, Ben Bradlee, and the 1971 publishing of the Pentagon Papers was so topical and important that he halted production on a delayed period film and rushed The Post to a Christmas 2017 release. The Post, a paradigm of stripped-down, streamlined narrative, became a must-see film of the time. It's easy to ignore flaws (there are a few) since The Post is generally exciting, a showcase for MerylStreep's greatest performance in at least a decade, maybe since Adaptation.

Graham's storyline carries the picture, and she's understated to great effect. Her relationship with Hanks' gruff Bradlee, who is quiet, deliberative, and harsh, is comfortable, lived-in, and humorous when they sometimes clash.

12. Road to Perdition, 2002

In Sam Mendes' vintage gangster picture, Hanks plays a seasoned crook with Paul Newman, Jennifer Jason Leigh, and a pre-Bond Daniel Craig. With this kind of skill both behind and in front of the camera,

Road to Perdition seemed to be one for the ages, but it ultimately seems too choreographed. It's simple to recommend, however, and its themes about dads and sons are especially moving. Road to Perdition looks stunning in almost every scene, due to Mendes' reunion with American Beauty cinematographer Conrad Hall.

13. Splash (1984)

Ron Howard's rom-com about an everyman and a mermaid stars Tom Hanks and Daryl Hannah. Splash was nominated for an Academy Award for Best Original Screenplay for being the first picture released under Disney's Touchstone division for older audiences. The clever writing is the most useful aspect here, mining an idea that might have been just adorable for typical rom-com misunderstandings and hijinks.

14. Saving Mr. Banks (2013)

Hanks co-stars with Emma Thompson in The Blind Side, director John Lee Hancock's award-winning, underappreciated family dramedy about the long road to the creation of the legendary 1964 musical Mary Poppins, centering on author P.L. Travers' tense relationship with Walt Disney.

Some reviews criticized the picture for being too exaggerated and cushioned from reality, yet Thompson and Hanks are captivating, and Saving Mr. Banks has an emotional hook that works much too well. This is the first time Walt Disney has been portrayed in a mainstream film; Disney CEO Bob Iger approached Hanks directly about the idea.

15. Elvis (2022)

Baz Luhrmann's greatest film since the magnificent Moulin Rouge! achieves all it has to do to commemorate pop music's pioneer for a contemporary audience. Elvis, like the Australian auteur's 2001 Oscar winner, is so lavish and dynamic that it would be mayhem if it weren't for superb performances and heart—which there is enough of.

Yes, it's a sequined cape biography, but the deliberate spectacle and sincere melodrama make it seem timeless. A vivacious Hanks chews the scenery as what is maybe his least sympathetic character ever; ultimately, this is Austin Butler's show—and what a spectacle it is. A new star is born.

16. Cast Away (2000)

This drama about a workaholic FedEx executive who becomes the lone survivor of a cargo jet catastrophe is one of the high points of inventive filmmaker Robert Zemeckis and Hanks' long-running professional partnership.

Hanks has stayed popular for decades, thanks in part to his willingness to take chances. Though Helen Hunt's minimal screen time improves Cast Away considerably, Hanks spends most of the film performing alongside a volleyball called Wilson. The fact that such a picture captivated people is without a doubt a credit to the skill involved. Cast Away made nearly $429 million worldwide, and Hanks was nominated for an Academy Award.

17. The Green Mile (film, 1999)

The Green Mile, one of the excellent Frank Darabont adaptations of Stephen King's writings, starring Tom Hanks and Michael Clarke Duncan in a narrative about strange happenings on a Depression-era death row. Despite lasting more than three hours, The Green Mile is engrossing and full of character. The film was nominated for four Academy Awards, including Best Picture, Best Supporting Actor (Duncan), Best Sound, and Best Adapted Screenplay.

18. Sleepless in Seattle, 1993

This swoon-worthy, often funny romantic comedy about a widower and a reporter who fall in love over the airwaves, stars Tom Hanks and Ryan, as well as director/co-writer Nora Ephron. Sleepless in Seattle was nominated for two Academy Awards and was a box office success, making almost ten times its budget worldwide.

19. A League of Their Own (film, 1992)

Penny Marshall's much-loved dramatized depiction of the real-life All-American Girls Professional Baseball League stars Tom Hanks, Geena Davis, Madonna, and Rosie O'Donnell. A League of Their Own is one of the most popular sports films of all time, and for good reason: it's entertaining for the whole family while also telling an inspirational underdog narrative. Baseball does not allow for tears!

20. Catch Me If You Can, 2002

Catch Me If You Can is a stylish, humorous, and heartwarming sort-of biopic based on the (much contested and disproven) memoirs of con ster Frank Abagnale Jr. and the FBI agent who chases him. It is an absolute triumph across the individual filmographies of Hanks, Spielberg, and Leonardo DiCaprio. It's a cat-and-mouse game at first, but it improves as it becomes more of a father-son narrative. Catch Me If You Can, wisely scheduled for a Christmas season 2002 release, resonated with a broad, intergenerational audience in a way that few films can.

21. The film Apollo 13 (1995).

This suspenseful recreation of the 1970 lunar trip is perhaps director Ron Howard's greatest work to date, and the producers went to great measures to make Apollo 13 scientifically correct as well as entertaining. Stars Tom Hanks, Kevin Bacon, Bill Paxton, Gary Sinise, and Ed Harris dedicated themselves to studying and experiencing as much as they could in preparation for their extremely technical parts, even dazzling NASA.

There were nine Academy Award nominations for Apollo 13—including Best Picture, which was won for Best Film Editing and Best Sound. It was a beautifully produced, visceral, and emotionally effective drama about real-life survival against all odds.

22. Captain Phillips (2013 film)

Technically immaculate and almost excruciating in terms of tension, this critical and financial success Captain Phillips brings Hanks together with Paul Greengrass, the director of United 93 and The Bourne Supremacy. It is based on the 2009 hijacking of the US containership Maersk Alabama by Somali pirates and the subsequent hostage situation. Captain Phillips' last moments include some of the beloved actor's best throw-down, tragic performances. It's the type of stuff that sticks with you and reminds you why this is one of our most popular performers.

23. Big (1988)

Even in 1988, this kind of body-swap comic premise seemed tired. Penny Marshall's Big, about a 12-year-old boy whose magical desire transforms him into a 30-year-old man, exceeded expectations thanks to a great story by Gary Ross and Anne Spielberg (focusing more on character than high jinks and yuks). Big, which starred Elizabeth Perkins and the underappreciated Robert Loggia, was a huge blockbuster and earned Hanks his first Oscar nomination for Best Actor. Big remains enthralling even after all these years.

24. Philadelphia, 1993

The extraordinarily humanistic Jonathan Demme's Oscar-winning drama Philadelphia had a major influence on pop culture and beyond two years after The Silence of the Lambs shattered box-office records and permanently entered the zeitgeist (and also garnered condemnation from activists). Hanks played a homosexual lawyer who is sacked from his firm once his AIDS diagnosis is revealed. Denzel Washington portrayed the attorney who represents him in court as he files a discrimination lawsuit.

25. Private Ryan's Revenge (1998)

There are two periods in the history of war films: before and after Saving Private Ryan. Saving Private Ryan is one of cinema's most important war films since Lewis Milestone's All Quiet on the Western Front (1930), which director Steven Spielberg credits as a major influence. The fighting sequences are as impressive for their technical mastery and realism (Spielberg reportedly did not plot the D-Day landing scene because he desired true spontaneity) as they are for being stomach-turning and, at times, nearly terrible to watch.

So many older World War II pictures appear antiquated and fake in comparison to the stark, marvelously immersive Saving Private Ryan. This video is very moving for soldiers and their families.

26. The Toy Story series (1995-2019)

Pixar's emotionally complex narrative of long-term friendship—and growing up—marked the beginning of a new era in animation. For a quarter-century, the series was a huge critical and commercial success.

Part three is the greatest of the Toy Story series. The surprisingly dark and sad diversions made in the third act are among the most daring and gratifying creative risks taken by Pixar artists. Toy Story 3 is a tremendously affecting picture, maybe particularly for millennial viewers who grew up with Andy. The fourth film is more contentious than the first, concluding with an uncomfortably adult tone.

27. Forrest Gump (film, 1994)

Hanks' eponymous hero Forrest Gump, who is slow-witted yet generous of heart, has grabbed the hearts of viewers all around the globe. Robert Zemeckis' truly American epic also finds the director at the pinnacle of his often-dominant career. The inventor employs amazing effects to convey the narrative of a nice guy who travels throughout the United States over many decades, endures loss, falls in love, and never gives up.

Forrest Gump nearly wasn't the picture we know today: Hanks had to pay for important sequences himself when the studio refused. The film was one of the greatest box-office blockbusters of the '90s, earning Best Picture, Best Director, and Hanks' second straight Best Actor Oscar. Forrest Gump is a film about bizarre alchemy that works like magic.

Chapter 12

Tom Hanks: With AI technology, I may feature in movies after death

Tom Hanks has shown interest in having his profession continue beyond his death via the use of artificial intelligence.

The Forrest Gump and Cast Away star said that the technology could be used to reproduce his visage, allowing him to continue appearing in films "from now until the kingdom comes."

He did admit that there were aesthetic and legal difficulties with the improvements.

Neil Tennant of the Pet Shop Boys has said that AI may be utilized by artists to finish tunes.

Hanks, 66, was questioned about the legal ramifications of the new technology on the most recent episode of The Adam Buxton podcast.

"This has always been lingering," he said. "The Polar Express was the first film in which we used a large amount of our data locked in a computer - literally what we looked like."

We predicted this would happen because we knew it was possible to create faces and characters out of zeros and ones from within a computer. Since then, it has only increased by a billion, and we can see it everywhere.

The Polar Express, which was released in 2004, was the first film to be animated using digital motion-capture technology.

In The Polar Express, Tom Hanks voiced various animated characters.
Hanks said that discussions are taking place in the film business about how to safeguard performers from the impacts of technology.

The legal repercussions of my face, voice, and everyone else's becoming our intellectual property are now being discussed in all of the guilds, agencies, and law companies, Hanks said.

It is now a true possibility that, if I so desired, I could come together and propose a run of seven films in which I would play a character who is 32 from this moment on until the end of time.

Now, anybody may rebuild oneself at any age utilizing artificial intelligence or deep fake technologies. Performances can go on forever, even if I am hit by a bus tomorrow and that's it.

If you don't grasp AI and deep fake, there won't be anything to let you know that it's not just you and me.

"And it will have some resemblance to reality." That is a creative problem, but it is also a legal one."

Previously, similar technology was employed in the last Indiana Jones film, in which Harrison Ford, 80, was "de-aged" for the opening scene.

The illusion of Indiana Jones in 1944 was created by combing through the old film of the younger Ford and comparing it to fresh footage.

Hanks said that technology advancements may result in an AI-generated version of himself participating in projects that he would not typically select.

People will undoubtedly be able to discern [that it's AI], but the real issue is whether they care. Some individuals will not care, and will not make that distinction."

Chapter 13

Tom Hanks joins Hollywood writers on strike: Find out the Truth

On Tuesday, May 16, 2023, the 66-year-old actor, who is presently on tour to promote his new book, announced his intention to join the strike in solidarity with Hollywood authors. The writers' organization has gone on strike in response to concerns about equitable remuneration in the streaming age.

He saw his sector as being at "an evolutionary crossroads."

According to Hanks, he would go on strike to support the writers' cause and is standing in sympathy with them.

On Monday, he spoke at a book event in Los Angeles about his novel, during which he linked the current strike to those of the 1980s.

Several actors and writers went on strike throughout the decade, and Hanks is said to have taken part in at least one of them.

The Cast Away star drew comparisons between streaming services and the advent of home video in the 1980s at the occasion.

The 1980 Hollywood actors' strike was about demands for a cut of the profits from

VHS and other media releases of films and TV shows.

Home video was the new thing that was on the way, according to Hanks. "That was because something new was on the way," he stated.

They anticipated a cash flow that had never been seen in the business before because of the invention of VHS. They were curious as to what it would be since it was arriving.

'I'm on strike,' says the striker.

According to Hanks, there are "economic realities" of streaming that will similarly affect the business of how video grew.

Let's identify the pie, he said, "because it's been about this idea that something new was coming down.

I think everyone is now aware of the financial realities of streaming. We are at a turning point in human development in terms of how that pie (would influence the business).

"And when I talk about the pie, I'm talking about the new place that society is in, where there are so many options for entertainment, that this 'new concept' is that we all now have to want to do something very unique, which used to be very standard in our lives."

"The unusual thing is that we drive away from home, arrive at a place at 7.45 p.m., park the car, buy a ticket, get a Diet Coke, and sit in a room full of strangers to watch a movie," he said.

That is no longer higher up the food chain than it formerly was.

"So, I'm a member of every guild there is, and I'm on strike because this has to be decided."

"Not just for the future of bread-and-butter issues that affect us all, but also for the arts and sciences of motion pictures."

13.1 What are the requirements?

The union is pushing for greater minimum wages, more writers per program, and less exclusivity on single projects, among other things, arguing that these conditions are required given the development of content during the streaming era.

Over 11,000 members of the Authors Guild of America (WGA) recently went on strike after discussions between studios and the authors, which started in March, failed to produce a new contract before the writers' existing pact ended.

Many TV series and films have already been impacted by the strikes, including:

• Stranger Things Season 5 • Yellowjackets Season 3 • The Handmaid's Tale Season 6

Other stars in Hollywood have endorsed the strikes as well.

This week, Jane Fonda said to Sky News that she and the other Book Club: The Next Chapter cast members are "very supportive" of the plot.

We can appreciate their decision to strike since today's entertainment industry is far more competitive than it was in the past.

The current strike has already had a substantial effect on various Hollywood films, as well as big events like the forthcoming Tony Awards and the 2023 MTV Movie and TV Awards.

Throughout the evening, Hanks revealed experiences from his long career that inspired the events and people in his book, which goes into the world of a multimillion-dollar superhero action film.

Previously, Hanks characterized the book as a "release from the never-ending pressure" of creating movies. He also said that several of the book's characters, including an eccentric director and conceited actor, were influenced by his personal experiences.

With Tom Hanks joining the striking writers, their cause gets a celebrity supporter. The resolution of this strike will not only influence the industry's day-to-day concerns but will also determine the future of motion picture arts and sciences. As Hollywood approaches a critical juncture, the union's demands take center stage, and the business prepares itself for an epochal shift.

Chapter 14

Tom Hanks's Health Situation

Tom Hanks seemed to have difficulty controlling his trembling hands at the recent 'Elvis' premiere, prompting some to speculate that he was ill.

Tom Hanks is one of Hollywood's most popular performers, and many people want to defend him passionately. He was one of the first celebrities to test positive for COVID-19, but he recovered well, and most people have not been worried about his health in the years following. Following the release of Elvis, many people have expressed worry regarding Tom's health.

Concerns about Tom's health arose when witnesses spotted him struggling to control trembling in his right hand while walking the red carpet at the Elvis premiere in Sydney, Australia. In the film, Tom portrays Colonel Tom Parker, the manager of the eponymous rock star.

While on the red carpet, he addressed the crowd, discussing what it was like to make the film in Australia.

Tom said, holding a microphone in his right hand, "There is no greater spot in the world to produce a motion picture than right here on the Gold Coast. I've produced movies in Berlin, Seattle, Los Angeles, New York, and Morocco. What distinguishes the Gold Coast from the others? Just two words. Dan

Murphy is not in any of the other cities. What a wonderful guy I got to know."

Tom's right hand started to tremble at this point, and he looked to be having difficulty controlling it. He ultimately put his left hand on top of his right hand, which was still holding the microphone, and then entirely switched hands. He then proceeded, claiming that he had a fantastic experience making the picture with his co-stars and director Baz Luhrmann.

Tom Hanks has seemed frail in recent events.
In addition to his trembling hands, fans have been worried about the actor since he has appeared at numerous recent Elvis-related events appearing incredibly

emaciated. Tom's weight has varied throughout his career, but some speculated that his suddenly slender physique may be an indicator of health difficulties that he has not publicly addressed.

Why Tom Hanks Felt Like "A Total Idiot" After Diabetic Diagnosis

In an unexpectedly open interview with Radio Times, Hanks called himself a "total idiot" for making a big health blunder that led to his diabetes diagnosis.

Continue reading to find out which bad habit the actor now greatly regrets and how he astonished fans by following a doctor's recommendations.

Hanks originally revealed his diabetes diagnosis in 2013.

In an appearance on the Late Show with David Letterman in 2013, Hanks said that learning he had diabetes was a great surprise—though it should have come as no surprise at all. 'You know those high blood sugar readings you've had since you were 36?' the doctor asked me when I saw him." You've completed your coursework! Young guy, you have type 2 diabetes," Hanks remarked.

Until that point, the Sleepless in Seattle actor had taken only minor dietary measures to prevent the course of his pre-diabetes. He told the Radio Times, "I believed I could get away with it by taking the buns off my cheeseburgers. Well, it takes a little more than that, I suppose.

He said he felt like a "total idiot" after receiving the diagnosis.

Hanks claims that his poor eating habits were a direct cause of his high blood sugar levels. "I'm part of the lazy American generation that has blindly kept dancing through the party and now finds ourselves with a malady," the actor said to Radio Times. "I was big. You've seen me in movies and are familiar with my appearance. "I was a complete moron."

Experts say that if you are pre-diabetic, as Hanks is, decreasing five to ten percent of your body weight may assist to reverse the course of your condition. According to Johns Hopkins Medicine, doing so reduces your chance of acquiring type 2 diabetes by 58%.

His doctor assured him that it was not too late to make things right.

Despite the severity of his diagnosis, Hanks claims his doctor remained hopeful that improvement was possible—but only if the actor made drastic adjustments to his health practices.Hanks said to Letterman in 2013: "My doctor says if I can get to a certain weight, I won't have type 2 diabetes any longer."

However, at the time, the Splash star was unconvinced that he could make major enough adjustments to cure his sickness. "I'm going to have type 2 diabetes then because there is no way I can weigh [what I weighed] in high school," he joked.

In Cannes, he highlighted his recent weight reduction.

Since that interview, it seems that the Forrest Gump actor has changed his mind. He no longer accepts his diabetes as inevitable and says he works hard to maintain a healthy weight and blood sugar levels. "I make an effort to exercise for an hour every day." He told Phoebe Robinson on the podcast Sooo Many White Guys in 2018: "That may be anything from a treadmill to a stroll or a trek with a dog, but it needs to be one hour every single day. "I watch what I eat to the point of boredom, and now and then I cheat to the point of self-loathing," he said, blaming his ailment on both heredity and "the miserable way of eating anything I had."

All of his hard work, though, seemed to have paid off. Fans observed Hanks looked thinner than ever when on the red carpet in Cannes for a screening of his new picture, Elvis. Though controlling weight is just one aspect of diabetes care, Hanks considers it a significant step in the right way.

Conclusion

Tom Hanks is one of the greatest directors and performers of all time, and he will undoubtedly remain an icon for future generations. He is a very successful actor, having attained superstardom with blockbuster films such as Forrest Gump, Cast Away, and Saving Private Ryan, as well as critical praise and massive popularity.

His career has covered all genres, and he has constantly delivered excellent performances and compelling storytelling. His contributions to movies have been much more extensive since he has also established himself as a recognized writer, producer, director, and philanthropist. Tom Hanks' films have not only received several accolades over the years, but they have also inspired and uplifted millions of moviegoers by allowing them to identify with the characters, themes, and messages in his films. His continuous success and wide-ranging effect reflect his long-lasting impact on society, entertainment, and art. Tom Hanks will remain a timeless gem in Hollywood and will continue to offer pleasure and inspiration to the globe via his films as an irreplaceable contribution to the film industry.

Tom Hanks' incredible achievements have gained him acclaim from spectators as well as recognition from other directors and performers. He has played classic characters like Woody and Buzz Lightyear, as well as Andrew Beckett and Mike Szymanski, like no other actor. His incredible flexibility and dedication to creating particularly powerful pictures and thought-provoking have secured his standing as a megastar.

Tom Hanks is one of the most well-known actors of all time, and for good reason: he is an indisputable star who has created a plethora of treasured memories for fans and continues to delight people with his amazing ability. His amazing career and effect on business and viewers throughout the globe will be remembered for a long time.